Greek Mythology
for Kids

Captivating Tales and Myths of Greek Gods,
Goddesses, Mythological Creatures,
Heroes, Kings, and Villains

Table of Contents

INTRODUCTION

In this book, you will discover the epic stories from Greek mythology. Be amazed by the many mighty gods, their incredible powers, and how they impacted some of the great heroes on their famous quests.

So, first things first, what do we mean when we say Greek mythology? *Mythology* is a collection of *myths*. These are old stories that have been changed over time to become fantastic and often supernatural in nature. While these myths might not be true, many of the people and places are real. And the ancient Greeks believed them. That is why they are still a very important part of history.

Prepare to dive into a world where monsters exist, good triumphs over evil, and gods and men live alongside one another.

Chapter 1: The Birth of the Gods

Before there was life, planets, or gods, there was only a vast nothingness. From that emptiness, the goddess known as *Chaos* was born. Afterward, three new *primordial deities* emerged. These gods existed at the beginning of time. *Gaia* was the goddess of Earth. *Tartarus* was the god of the *underworld*, where the souls of the dead went. And there was the god of love, *Eros*. Between them, Chaos and Gaia were able to create the universe.

Chaos gave birth to darkness, *Erebus (eh-ruh-buhs)*, and his sister, the night, *Nyx (nix)*. Erebus and Nyx then gave birth to the air, *Aether*, and the day, *Hemera*. Nyx was feared by many and decided to create a large, terrifying family of her own. She gave birth to death (*Thanos*), pain (*Oizys*), revenge (*Nemesis*), sleep (*Hypnos*), dreams (*Oneiroi*), blame (*Momos*), old age (*Geras*), doom (*Ker*), and deceit (*Apate*). Nyx also gave birth to many more deities, including the *Hesperides (heh-sper-ih-deez)*, who were known as the "daughters of the evening."

Fun Fact: Today, we have adopted some of these Greek names into English. For example, we still refer to someone's enemy as their nemesis. Putting someone into a sleep-like trance is called hypnosis.

Fun Fact: The Marvel supervillain, Thanos, was based on the Greek god of the same name!

Nyx was not the only goddess having lots of children. Gaia gave birth to *Ouranos* (or Uranus), who was the god of the sky. Gaia and Ouranos became husband and wife. They gave birth to three *Cyclopes*, who were giant one-eyed monsters, and three *Hecatonchires (hek-a-ton-kereez)*, who were giant creatures who had fifty heads and one hundred arms!

Ouranos was threatened by the Cyclopes and the Hecatonchires' great power, so he decided he would lock all six sons inside of Gaia. After this, Gaia and Ouranos gave birth to the twelve *Titans*. These were six sons and six daughters. Ouranos was less afraid of these children, so he allowed them to remain free. This proved to be a big mistake.

Gaia found it painful to contain her other children inside her. She asked the Titans to help them escape. When Ouranos next came down to Earth, the Titans pinned him down at all four corners of the world. One of the Titan brothers, *Kronos*, then wielded a *sickle* (a type of curved blade used in farming) and castrated Ouranos. Ouranos no longer had the power to rule over the heavens, and the Titans took control. Kronos became the supreme deity and ruler.

Kronos with the sickle.
(https://commons.wikimedia.org/wiki/File:Saturnus_fig274.png)

When castrating Ouranos, his blood fell onto Gaia, which created more children. One hundred giants, the *Gigantes*, and the ash-tree *nymphs* (female deities associated with nature) called *Meliae* were born. The three *Furies*, who were the goddesses of vengeance, were also born. The final child born to Ouranos and Gaia was the goddess of beauty, *Aphrodite*. Aphrodite was born when Ouranos's castrated body parts fell into the ocean.

Sadly, when Kronos became the supreme deity, he was not any better than his father. He was just as cruel. He reimprisoned the Cyclopes and Hecatonchires in the deepest part of the underworld.

Fun Fact: The underworld, Tartarus, was guarded by a female dragon monster called Campe (cam-pay).

Kronos married his Titaness sister *Rhea*. Together, they had five children. Kronos was fearful that the past would repeat itself. He did not want to be overthrown by his offspring. So, he decided to *devour* (eat) his babies.

Rhea was very sad to lose her children. When she gave birth to her sixth son, *Zeus*, she decided to trick Kronos. Rhea hid Zeus on the island of Crete with the nymphs. Then, she wrapped a baby-sized stone in blankets and gave it to Kronos instead. Kronos greedily swallowed the stone, thinking it was the baby.

Rhea gives Kronos the stone.
(https://commons.wikimedia.org/wiki/File:Rh%C3%A9a
pr%C3%A9sentant_une_pierre_emmaillot%C3%A9e_
%C3%A0_Cronos_dessin_du_bas-relief_d%27un_autel_romain.jpg)

While in Crete, Zeus was raised by two nymphs, *Adrasteia (a-dra-stee-a)* and *Ida*. He grew strong from drinking their goat's milk, which was named *Amalthea (a-mal-thee-a)*.

Zeus did not know his own strength as a boy. He accidentally broke off one of Amalthea's horns when playing. As an apology, he blessed the horn so it would provide its owner with anything they wanted.

Fun Fact: The horn became known as the cornucopia, which was a symbol to the ancient Greeks for abundance (having lots of something) and nourishment (being well-fed). Because of this, food would often be served in horn-shaped pottery at feasts in ancient Greece.

Zeus being nurtured by Amalthea's milk.
(https://commons.wikimedia.org/wiki/File:Nicolas_Poussin_-_Jupiter_enfant_nourri_par_la_ch%C3%A8vre_Amalth%C3%A9e.jpg)

When Zeus became a man, he asked his future wife, the goddess of wisdom, *Metis*, how he could defeat Kronos. Metis told Zeus he should disguise himself as a cupbearer and pour Kronos wine that had been poisoned. The plan worked, and Kronos threw up the five children he had swallowed: *Hades*, *Poseidon*, *Demeter*, *Hestia*, and *Hera*. The five siblings joined Zeus to become the *Olympians* and overthrow Kronos. However, Kronos had the support of his own siblings. A very long war between the Titans and the Olympians began.

Fun Fact: The Olympians were named this because they lived on Mount Olympus.

Bust of Zeus.
(https://commons.wikimedia.org/wiki/File:Zeus_Otricoli_Pio-Clementino_Inv257.jpg)

Chapter 1 Activity

Can you match the god to the relevant phrase about them?

Zeus	One-eyed giants
Gaia	A goat who nourished Zeus
Kronos	The goddess of Earth
Ouranos	The leader of the Olympians
Cyclopes	The mother of Zeus and the Olympians
Hecatonchires	The father of Kronos and the Titans
Rhea	Ate his children
Amalthea	They have one hundred hands and arms

Chapter 1 Answer

Cyclopes	One-eyed giants
Gaia	The goddess of Earth
Zeus	The leader of the Olympians
Amalthea	A goat who nourished Zeus
Rhea	The mother of Zeus and the Olympians
Ouranos	The father of Kronos and the Titans
Kronos	Ate his children
Hecatonchires	They have one hundred hands and arms

Chapter 2: Titans and Giants

For ten years, the Olympians and the Titans fought in a war called the Titanomachy. Just when it seemed like the Olympians were going to lose the war, Zeus followed the advice of Gaia. He freed the Cyclopes and the Hecatonchires from their prison. As a thank you, the Cyclopes made a thunderbolt for Zeus to use as a weapon. They also gave Hades a helmet that would make the wearer invisible. And they gave Poseidon a trident (a type of spear with three prongs—points). With these new weapons, the Olympians were more powerful than ever.

A modern illustration of a Cyclops.
(https://pixabay.com/illustrations/cyclops-creature-eye-longleat-5743904/)

The Cyclopes weren't the only ones who were grateful to Zeus for setting them free. The Hecatonchires also helped the Olympians win. During one battle, they set a trap for Kronos and the Titans. Once the Titans were in a valley below the mountains, the Hecatonchires used their one hundred hands to quickly throw boulders on the Titans below. The Titans were finally defeated.

All the Titans were jailed in Tartarus and guarded by the Hecatonchires, although a few eventually earned their freedom.

Fun Fact: Before their defeat, the Titans lived at their headquarters on Mount Othrys.

The Olympian brothers then divided up the universe by drawing straws. Zeus was the king of the humans and gods, as well as the sky. Poseidon ruled the seas. Hades drew the short straw. He would be in charge of the underworld.

The Titans weren't the only children of Gaia and Ouranos that the Olympians would have to defeat. They also had to fight the Gigantes in a series of battles known as the Gigantomachy.

There were many different battles during the Gigantomachy. The giant Enceladus (en-seh-la-dos) was defeated by the goddess of war, Athena. Enceladus was one of the most powerful Gigantes. It was decided that he would take over control of the oceans if the Gigantes won the Gigantomachy.

Enceladus wanted to marry Athena, an idea that was considered offensive and impossible because Athena was a virgin. It was seen as a threat, and the gods needed to defeat him. During the fight, Athena buried Enceladus under Mount Etna in Sicily. Enceladus is immortal, which means he cannot die. According to legend, he remains trapped under Mount Etna. It is believed that his anger and movements beneath the volcano are what cause it to erupt.

Another famous fight was between Poseidon and the Gigantes Polybotes (pah-leh-boh-teez). During a battle, Polybotes attempted to escape, but Poseidon chased him through the ocean until they reached the island of Kos. Poseidon broke off part of the island and threw it at Polybotes. The rock hit the giant and buried him underneath. This became a new island called Nisyros.

Another Gigantes, Mimas (mai-mas), was defeated by Hephaestus, the god of fire. Hephaestus killed Mimas by throwing red-hot, flaming metal at him and pouring molten iron on him.

Zeus was, of course, involved in many of the battles during the Gigantomachy. His half-mortal son, Hercules (the Romanized version of the Greek Heracles), was also integral in helping the Olympians defeat the Gigantes. In one battle, he helped the goddess Hera defeat the giant Porphyrion (poor-fe-ree-on). Zeus cast a spell on Porphyrion during the fight so that he fell in love with Hera. While he

Poseidon fighting Polybotes
(https://commons.wikimedia.org/wiki/File:Poseidon_Polybotes_Cdm_Paris_573.jpg)

was distracted by Hera, Zeus threw a thunderbolt at him, and Hercules killed him with an arrow.

Fun Fact: In ancient drawings of the Gigantes, they are often shown with snakes instead of legs!

If fighting the Titans and Gigantes for control of the universe wasn't difficult enough, the Olympians also had to defeat another one of Gaia's children. Typhoeus (tai-foe-uhs) or Typhon was the deadliest monster in Greek mythology. He was a fire-breathing dragon with one hundred heads, which never had to sleep. He had the body of a man, but he had snakes for legs and hands.

Fun Fact: Gaia gave birth to Typhon to punish Zeus for locking the Titans in Tartarus.

Typhon and his wife, Echidna (eh-kid-nah), were known as the mother and father of all monsters. Their three most famous children were the Sphinx, the Nemean Lion, and Cerberus. The Sphinx was a creature with a human head, the body of a lion, and the wings of a falcon. It protected the city of Thebes and killed anyone who could not solve its riddles. The Nemean Lion was a lion with armored fur that could not be pierced by weapons. It had claws that were sharper than swords. Cerberus was a dog with three heads that guarded the gates of the underworld.

Fun Fact: Fluffy, the three-headed dog in the Harry Potter books and films, is based on Cerberus. Just like Fluffy, the only way to get past Cerberus was to play him music!

Typhon was so frightening to look at that the Olympians all ran away in fear. However, Zeus decided to fight Typhon after Athena said he would be a coward if he ran like the others. Zeus injured Typhon with his sickle, and they began to fight in hand-to-hand combat. Typhon gained the upper hand when he managed to cut Zeus's tendons.

Typhon left the wounded Zeus in a cave with his dragon sister to keep an eye on him. Zeus's son Hermes came to his rescue and treated his injuries, sewing the tendons back together. When Zeus regained his strength, he returned to fight Typhon, throwing hundreds of thunderbolts at the monster and driving him into Tartarus. Zeus then moved Mount Etna to cover the entrance so that Typhon could not escape.

Pottery showing Zeus fighting Typhon.
(https://commons.wikimedia.org/wiki/File:Zeus_Typhon_Staatliche_Antikensammlungen_596.jpg)

Chapter 2 Activity

1. Where was the "headquarters" of the Titans?

2. What were the gifts that the Cyclopes gave to Zeus and his brothers, Poseidon and Hades?

3. How did Poseidon defeat the giant Polybotes?

4. How did Athena defeat the giant Enceladus?

5. How did Zeus destroy Typhon?

Chapter 2 Answer

1. Where was the "headquarters" of the Titans? Mount Othrys.

2. What were the gifts that the Cyclopes gave to Zeus and his brothers, Poseidon and Hades? Zeus was given thunderbolts. Poseidon was given a trident. Hades was given a helmet of invisibility.

3. How did Poseidon defeat the giant Polybotes? By throwing a piece of an island at him.

4. How did Athena defeat the giant Enceladus? By burying him under Mount Etna.

5. How did Zeus destroy Typhon? With thunderbolts.

Chapter 3: The Olympians

We've already heard a little bit about the Olympians. Let's get to know them more. There were twelve Olympians that lived on Mount Olympus.

The leader of the Olympians and the ruler of the heavens was Zeus. Zeus could control the weather and used thunderbolts when fighting.

In drawings and statues of Zeus, he is often portrayed holding thunderbolts. Sometimes, he is shown holding a *scepter* (a type of staff or stick held by kings to show they are the ruler) or wearing a crown of leaves from his sacred oak tree. Zeus is almost always shown with a big beard, which demonstrates his masculinity.

A statue of Zeus.
(https://commons.wikimedia.org/wiki/File:Jupiter_Smyrna_Louvre_Ma13.jpg)

Although Zeus was the king of the gods, his siblings did not always bow down to his control. They believed he was too proud and wanted to teach him a lesson. When he was asleep, they tied him up and stole his thunderbolts. Zeus was able to escape with the help of a nymph. He punished his rebellious siblings. After this, they promised they would never question his rule again.

Fun Fact: There are many similarities between Zeus and the gods of other religions. Perhaps the best-known gods that resemble Zeus are the Norse gods Thor and Odin, who have made appearances in many superhero films.

Zeus had many wives and affairs. Zeus also had lots of children. Zeus would even have love affairs with human women who would then give birth to half-human, half-god children (demigods). Zeus had so many children and relationships that it is practically impossible to list them all!

When Zeus's first wife, Metis, became pregnant, he was worried that the child would grow up to be a threat to him. So, just like his father before him, Zeus decided he would swallow the child. However, he went one step further than Kronos. He decided that he would not wait for the child to be born and swallowed his pregnant wife instead! Luckily, this did not stop his child from being born. His daughter Athena popped out of his forehead, fully grown and wearing armor.

Athena was the goddess of wisdom and war, but she was also a virgin goddess. She was often associated with handicrafts, such as weaving. Even though she was a war god, she was often considered to be peaceful. The other gods respected and feared her, and they would come to her for advice. Athena was the patron god of the city of

Athens. It is unclear which name came first. Because she was a virgin deity, Athena did not have any children or husbands.

Athena is often shown as being very beautiful but unsmiling and powerful. She is either shown with fine fabrics draped over her or in full armor. When Athena is shown with armor, she is often holding an *aegis* (shield) that belonged to Zeus, which she would borrow. On the aegis was the head of the *Gorgon Medusa*—a mythical beast with snakes for hair that would turn people who looked in its eyes to stone.

A statue of Athena.
(https://pixabay.com/photos/athens-greece-hellas-statue-greek-6784641/)

Zeus's most famous wife was the goddess Hera. Hera was the goddess of marriage and is associated with women, children, and family. Zeus tricked Hera into their marriage by transforming himself into a cuckoo bird. He knew that Hera loved animals, so he flew up to her, pretending to be injured. When Hera held the cuckoo close to her chest, he turned back into human form. Hera was ashamed of being tricked and agreed to marry Zeus.

Fun Fact: Although Zeus happily cheated on Hera, he would not tolerate any man trying to woo her. One unlucky soul who tried was tied to a wheel of fire that would spin and burn for all eternity.

Hera was very jealous of Zeus's many affairs and would often punish the women. When Zeus had relationships with mortal women, he would have to disguise himself since humans would die if they saw a god in their true form. Hera would often trick Zeus into showing his human lovers his true self so they would die. She would also punish any women who claimed to be as beautiful as her by banishing them to the underworld.

Statues of Zeus and Hera.

In statues and drawings, Hera would often be shown alongside her husband. As the queen of the gods, she is sometimes depicted wearing a crown and holding a scepter with a cuckoo on top of it.

Zeus's brother Poseidon was the god of the sea. Like Hades in the underworld, he did not live on Mount Olympus. Instead, he chose to live in his golden kingdom under the sea. Poseidon was an angry god, and this would often account for the unpredictability and danger of the ocean.

Fun Fact: In the 1989 animated Disney movie The Little Mermaid, Ariel's father, King Triton, is influenced by Poseidon and his Roman counterpart, Neptune.

Much like his brother, Poseidon is often shown as having a big beard and piercing eyes. He also had a weakness for women. In total, Poseidon fathered fourteen children. If he couldn't win a woman over with romance, he would trick them or use violence to get his way.

When Poseidon met Medusa, she was not a Gorgon. She was a beautiful mortal woman. However, after he took her against her will, Athena was enraged and turned the woman into a monster.

Another woman Poseidon tricked was the goddess *Demeter*. She turned into a horse to try to escape his advances, but he transformed into a stallion. From this encounter, she gave birth to a nymph and a talking horse.

Fun Fact: Poseidon was the creator of horses.

As well as physically resembling Zeus, Poseidon is often shown riding in a chariot, and he is usually holding his trident. By hitting a rock with the trident, Poseidon created the first horse.

Poseidon with his trident.

Demeter was the goddess of agriculture and fertility. Although she was the goddess of the harvest, she was also associated with law and the circle of life and death.

Fun Fact: Demeter is nicknamed "Mother Nature."

Demeter had one child with Zeus, a daughter called *Persephone*. Persephone was a virgin deity who was young and very beautiful. This caught the attention of the king of the underworld, Hades. He fell in love with Persephone as soon as he saw her. While Persephone was picking flowers, she was lured away from her mother by the most incredible and sweet-smelling flowers. As she bent down to pick one, a huge hole opened up to reveal the underworld. Hades came riding out of it in a giant chariot pulled by black stallions, and he kidnapped Persephone.

Demeter was heartbroken when she discovered Persephone was missing. She searched everywhere for her daughter. Because she was so focused on finding her daughter, Demeter forgot to take care of the land. Crops began to die, and the land became inhospitable and barren.

Zeus realized Demeter needed to take care of the land. Otherwise, life on Earth would end. He had to intervene and try to return Persephone to her mother. However, this proved to be more difficult than anticipated. While in the underworld, Persephone ate some pomegranate seeds. In Greek mythology, anyone who ate the fruit of their captor would be forever bound to them. This meant that no matter what, Persephone would be tied to the underworld.

Eventually, it was agreed that Persephone would spend half of the year on Earth with her mother and the other half in the underworld with Hades. When Persephone returned to her mother, the Earth would experience spring and summer. Nature bloomed because Demeter was happy. But in autumn and winter, the leaves would fall, and the land would become cold. This was when Persephone returned to the underworld. Persephone was very unhappy as a captive in the beginning. But she grew to love Hades, and she was happy living in the underworld with him as his wife.

Fun Fact: While Hades and Persephone were related to the Olympians, they are not always counted among the twelve Olympian gods. This is because they lived in the underworld, not on Mount Olympus. Interestingly, although Poseidon did not live on Mount Olympus, he is still usually considered to be one of the twelve Olympians.

A statue of Demeter

The other male Olympians aren't quite as famous as their brothers. These were *Apollo, Ares, Hermes,* and *Hephaestus.* Apollo was the god of the sun and light, but he had many other roles too. He was associated with music, poetry, beauty, farming, plagues, archery, knowledge, truth, and healing. He was Zeus's son from one of his many affairs. Apollo was loved by men and women and had many romantic relationships with both. Sadly, he was not very lucky, and most of his relationships did not end well.

Fun Fact: Apollo is the only important Greek god whose name is the same in Roman mythology.

Ares was the male god of war. Unlike his female counterpart, Athena, Ares represented the deadly and violent side of war. Because of this, he was not well-liked. He is usually shown in armor and carries weapons while riding in a four-horse chariot.

Hermes delivered messages for the gods. He was the only Olympian who could cross the line between the living and the dead. He was also a prankster who enjoyed tricking people. In spite of this, he was adored by the other gods. Hermes is usually depicted with wings on his helmet, shoes, and staff.

A drawing of Hermes.
(https://commons.wikimedia.org/wiki/File:Hermes_-_Greek_mythology_systematized_(1880)_(14723236766).jpg)

Hephaestus was the god of fire. Because of this, he was the patron god of blacksmiths and other craftsmen. He was also often associated with volcanoes. Hephaestus was the ugliest of the Olympians. He was not considered physically perfect like the other gods. He was crippled and had a limp. Hephaestus was the son of Hera and Zeus. Hera was not a loving mother. She was disgusted by his bad looks. Despite his appearance, Hephaestus was married to the most beautiful goddess of all, the goddess of beauty, Aphrodite.

Although Aphrodite was married to Hephaestus, she was not faithful to him and was romantically involved with other Olympians. She was not only the goddess of beauty but also of fertility and love. Aphrodite was physically perfect and was usually depicted as naked.

The final two Olympian goddesses were *Artemis* and *Hestia*. Artemis was the goddess of the moon and hunting. She was also the virgin goddess of chastity. She is depicted as a young and beautiful woman. She usually wears a long gown or carries a bow and arrow. Artemis fiercely protected her purity and would use violence to do so. When any men tried to bed her, she would kill them.

The final Olympian in this chapter, Hestia, is probably the least well-known Olympian since she is not in many stories. She was the goddess of the *hearth* or fireplace. This meant she usually stayed at the gods' home and looked after the fire. She was very modest and peaceful. Hestia chose to stay out of the drama, unlike the other gods and goddesses. Like many of the other Olympian goddesses, Hestia was a virgin.

Chapter 3 Activity

Complete the sentences below.

1. Athena was born _____.

    a) in the sea   b) from Zeus's head   c) by an owl

2. _____ was the god of the seas.

    a) Zeus   b) Hades   c) Poseidon

3. The most beautiful goddess was_____.

    a) Aphrodite   b) Demeter   c) Athena

4. _____ captured Persephone and took her to live in the underworld.

    a) Hades   b) Hermes   c) Zeus

5. Persephone's mother _____ was heartbroken and looked everywhere for her.

    a) Hera   b) Hestia   c) Demeter

6. Athena was so upset with Poseidon for cheating that she turned the beautiful _____ into a monster.

    a) Artemis   b) Medusa   c) Aphrodite

7. Hermes was a messenger god; he had _____.

    a) wings on his clothing   b) a limp   c) a helmet of invisibility

8. Zeus tricked his wife Hera by turning into a _____.

    a) stallion   b) dog   c) cuckoo bird

Chapter 3 Answer

1. Athena was born from Zeus's head. **(b)**

2. Poseidon was the god of the seas. **(c)**

3. The most beautiful goddess was Aphrodite. **(a)**

4. Hades captured Persephone and took her to live in the underworld. **(a)**

5. Persephone's mother Demeter was heartbroken and looked everywhere for her. **(c)**

6. Athena was so upset with Poseidon for cheating that she turned the beautiful Medusa into a monster. **(b)**

7. Hermes was a messenger god; he had wings on his clothing. **(a)**

8. Zeus tricked his wife Hera by turning into a cuckoo bird. **(c)**

Chapter 4: Prometheus and the Cataclysm

In this chapter, you will hear the tale of Prometheus (pro-mee-thay-uhs) and how he caused the Great Cataclysm, a huge and destructive disaster. Prometheus was a Titan. However, during the Titanomachy, he and his brother, Epimetheus (eh-pee-mee-thay-uhs), supported Zeus and fought against the Titans.

The good relationship between Zeus and Prometheus did not last long. Prometheus believed that Zeus was an unfair god to the humans. He thought the gods should share more with them. Zeus once asked Prometheus to divide the meat from an ox between the gods and the mortals. Prometheus played a trick on him. Instead of splitting the meat equally, he covered the bones in fat and the meat in the ox's insides. Zeus believed the fatty pile was the best one, so he chose the bones. From that day forward, humans would only have to sacrifice the bones to the gods and could keep the meat.

Zeus did not like being made a fool. He wanted to punish the humans for this. So, he did not share the ability to make fire with them. Prometheus did not think something so valuable should belong to only the gods, so he stole the fire from them and gave it to the humans.

To honor the gift of fire, the people of Athens started a new tradition. They would run a relay race while passing a flaming torch. The winning team would then light the ceremonial fire.

Fun Fact: This is the origin story of the opening ceremony of the Olympic Games and the relay race.

As you can imagine, Zeus was furious at being betrayed by Prometheus again. He decided he would punish not only Prometheus but also the humans. Prometheus's punishment was a cruel one. Zeus chained him to a stone on a mountain so he could not move. He also sent an eagle to torture him. Every day, the eagle would eat Prometheus's liver. Because Prometheus was immortal, he could not die. His organs and skin would heal, and the eagle would come back the next day.

Zeus's punishment for humanity was much more elaborate. He went to Hephaestus and asked him to create a new creature that was very beautiful and cunning. The other gods provided their own enticing gifts to make the creature even more seductive to the humans. The creature they made was called Pandora, and she was the first woman.

The gods gave Pandora a box filled with evil things that would hurt humanity if it was opened. Inside the box were things like plagues, famine, and diseases.

Zeus sent Pandora to Earth to be Epimetheus's wife. Although Prometheus had told his brother never to accept a gift from Zeus, Epimetheus was won over by Pandora's beauty. He married her.

Pandora did not know what the box contained. One day, she decided to peek inside. As soon as she opened the box, all the horrible things came out. Realizing her mistake, she tried to close it. The only thing left in the box was hope. The Greeks believed that is why hope is the last thing to die in humans.

The people of Earth became corrupted by the contents of the box. They also misused the gift of fire. Zeus decided they had not learned their lesson. He planned to wipe out humanity and start again. Much like the Christian God in the New Testament, Zeus decided he would send a great flood to destroy everything on Earth.

The only humans Zeus spared were Deucalion (Dew-kay-lee-on), who was Prometheus's son, and his wife Pyrrha (pee-rah), who was the daughter of Epimetheus and Pandora. Prometheus was the god of foresight. He warned his son of the impending cataclysm (a great disaster). Like Noah in the Bible, Deucalion built a boat to escape the flood. However, he did not have enough space for the animals. Only the birds and aquatic creatures survived.

Despite his feud with Prometheus, Zeus decided to spare the two survivors. He believed they were pure of heart and godly. After nine days and nights, the floodwaters began to go down, and new plants began to grow again.

Deucalion and Pyrrha prayed to Zeus and thanked him for sparing them. He told them he would grant them one wish for their devotion. They asked him to repopulate the earth again. Zeus answered them with a riddle. He said they must throw their mother's bones behind their backs. Deucalion and Pyrrha understood the riddle. They knew the bones he was talking about were actually the stones that were the

31

backbone of Mother Earth. Every rock that Deucalion threw created a new man. Every stone that Pyrrha threw created a new woman.

So, while humanity did not escape Zeus's wrath, it was again reborn into a new era. The same can be said for Prometheus. He did not have to suffer his torment for all eternity. He was eventually freed by none other than Zeus's own son, Hercules.

A painting of Pandora.

Zeus agreed that Prometheus could remain free. But Prometheus would have to wear a reminder of his punishment. Zeus turned the chains Prometheus had been bound with into a ring that Prometheus could never take off.

Fun Fact: Humans began to create and wear rings of their own to show solidarity with Prometheus. After all, he was humanity's friend and the savior of mankind.

Hercules freeing Prometheus
(https://commons.wikimedia.org/wiki/File:Prometheus_and_Hercules.jpg)

Chapter 4 Activity

Can you fill in the blanks and complete the story?

Prometheus _____ fire from the gods and _____ to mankind. Then, Zeus _____ him by chaining him to a _____ on a mountain where an _____ would peck and eat his liver.

Zeus also punished the humans by creating _____ the first woman. She had a _____ filled with lots of terrible things like famine, plagues, and diseases. By the time she closed it again, only _____ was left inside.

The humans still had not learned their lesson. So, Zeus decided to send a _____ to wipe out humanity. The only humans to survive were Deucalion and Pyrrha because _____ warned them. After _____ days and nights, the water began to recede, and new life grew.

Zeus decided to grant one wish to Deucalion and Pyrrha. They wished for _____ to be reborn. To do this, Zeus told them they had to throw _____ behind their backs. They knew this meant they should throw _____ behind them. A new _____ was created when Deucalion threw his, and a new _____ was created when Pyrrha threw hers.

Prometheus <u>stole</u> fire from the gods and <u>gave it</u> to mankind. Then, Zeus <u>punished</u> him by chaining him to a <u>stone</u> on a mountain where an <u>eagle</u> would peck and eat his liver.

Zeus also punished the humans by creating <u>Pandora</u>, the first woman. She had a <u>box</u> filled with lots of terrible things like famine, plagues, and diseases. By the time she closed it again, only <u>hope</u> was left inside.

The humans still had not learned their lesson. So, Zeus decided to send a <u>flood</u> to wipe out humanity. The only humans to survive were Deucalion and Pyrrha because <u>Prometheus</u> warned them. After <u>nine</u> days and nights, the water began to recede, and new life grew.

Zeus decided to grant one wish to Deucalion and Pyrrha. They wished for <u>humanity</u> to be reborn. To do this, Zeus told them they had to throw <u>the bones of their mother</u> behind their backs. They knew this meant they should throw <u>rocks or stones</u> behind them. A new <u>man</u> was created when Deucalion threw his, and a new <u>woman</u> was created when Pyrrha threw hers.

Chapter 5: The Twelve Labors of Hercules

Hercules is one of the most famous Greek heroes. He was the son of Zeus and a mortal princess named *Alcmene (al-kay-mee-nee)*. Hera was furious when she learned that Zeus had another affair. She cast a spell so that Hercules would not inherit the rule of *Mycenae (mai-see-nee)* as Zeus had planned. Instead, a much weaker mortal, *Eurystheus (yo-ris-tay-uhs)*, would be king.

When Hercules was born, Hera sent two snakes to his crib to strangle him. However, even as a baby, Hercules was very strong. This was because he was a *demigod* (half-man, half-god). He bravely fought off the attack and survived.

Fun Fact: Hercules is so famous he even has his own movies! Disney released the animated movie Hercules in 1997.

A statue of Hercules.

As Hercules grew up, he became even stronger. He would often accidentally kill animals with his impressive strength. Unfortunately, Hera wasn't finished tormenting him. One day, she played a cruel trick on him. She cast a spell so that he would see what she wanted him to see. So, instead of seeing his loving family, Hercules saw a bunch of angry snakes. He killed them. When Hercules realized they were actually his wife and children, he was heartbroken. He went to the *Oracle of Delphi* so she could tell Hercules his *prophecy* (prediction of the future).

The Oracle told him that he could repent and make up for his sins. To do so, he had to serve King Eurystheus for twelve years and complete twelve labors for him. Once the twelve labors were finished, Hercules would be granted immortality and become a god.

Fun Fact: Originally, there were only meant to be ten labors, but the king found an excuse for there to be two more.

Eurystheus decided to make the tasks especially difficult. Perhaps this was because he knew that Hercules was the true heir to the throne.

The Nemean Lion

We have already mentioned the fearsome Nemean Lion and how it was more than just a regular lion. Hercules's first task was to kill the lion. It had been terrorizing the town of *Nemea* and kidnapping women. When the men tried to rescue the women, they would be eaten alive!

Fighting a regular lion would have been hard enough, but the Nemean Lion was even harder! Hercules soon realized his arrows would not work. The lion had armored fur that could not be pierced by weapons. He also had to watch out for its claws, which were sharper than swords. Hercules went to the lion's den and blocked all of the exits so it could not escape. He then snuck up on the lion and hit it with his club. He stunned the lion before strangling it with his bare hands.

Fun Fact: Afterward, Hercules wore the lion's impenetrable skin as armor.

A statue of Hercules and the Nemean Lion.
(https://pixabay.com/photos/statue-of-hercules-art-monument-2531191/)

The Lernaean Hydra

The next monster Hercules had to defeat had been made by Hera just to kill him. The *Lernaean Hydra (ler-nee-an Hi-drah)* lived in a swamp in *Lerna* and had nine heads. One of these heads was immortal. The Hydra looked a bit like a dragon with poisonous snakeheads.

Hercules began to cut the heads off the Hydra. But he was horrified to discover that for every head he cut off, two new ones would appear in its place. The more he fought, the stronger it got!

He realized he couldn't defeat it alone. He asked his nephew *Iolaus (eye-oh-lawhs)* to help. Iolaus had the great idea that they should *cauterize* the wounds with fire so the Hydra could not grow new heads. His plan worked, and the two were able to defeat the monster together.

Fun Fact: Eurystheus told Hercules that this labor did not count since he had help.

A drawing of Hercules fighting the Lernaean Hydra.
(https://commons.wikimedia.org/wiki/File:Hercules_
and_the_Hydra_of_Lerna_LACMA_65.37.9.jpg)

The Ceryneian Hind

The third task Hercules was given was to capture the *Ceryneian (se-re-neen-yan) Hind*. The Ceryneian Hind was a sacred deer with golden antlers. It belonged to the goddess Artemis. The deer was incredibly fast. It could even outrun arrows! Eurystheus and Hera decided to give

Hercules this task. If he was able to catch the deer, it would anger Artemis, and she would punish him.

Hercules tracked the deer for a whole year before he was finally able to get close enough to capture it while it was asleep. When Artemis appeared in front of Hercules, he begged for her forgiveness and explained why he had taken her deer. Instead of being mad, she gave him permission to take it to Eurystheus as long as he released it afterward.

When Eurystheus saw the deer, he proclaimed it was now his property. To keep his promise to Artemis, Hercules played a trick on the king. He told the king he should return home with the deer. He knew that it would easily escape the king and run back to Artemis.

A drawing of Hercules catching the Ceryneian Hind.

The Erymanthian Boar

Hercules's next task was to capture the *Erymanthian (airy-man-thee-an) Boar*. This was a man-eating wild boar, a type of pig with tusks. It lived on *Mount Erymanthos*.

Fun Fact: The Erymanthian Boar also belonged to Artemis.

On his way to capture the boar, Hercules stopped to see his *centaur* friend. A centaur has the lower body of a horse and the upper body of a man. Hercules's friend told him he could capture the boar by trapping it in snow. When Hercules returned with the boar, the king was so afraid that he hid. He even told Hercules to take it back!

A painting of Hercules scaring Eurystheus with the Erymanthian Boar.
(https://commons.wikimedia.org/wiki/File:Italian_School_-_Hercules_
Terrifying_King_Eurytheus_with_the_Erymanthian_Boar_-_108842_-_National_Trust.jpg)

The Stables of Augeas

Eurystheus was growing annoyed at Hercules always besting him and succeeding in his tasks. So, he decided that he would choose something that did not test Hercules's strength or intelligence. Instead, it would humiliate him. Hercules's fifth task was to clean a massive amount of horse manure from the *Stables of Augeas (awh-gee-uhs)* in just one day.

Hercules asked for a tenth of the horses if he was successful. The king agreed. Of course, Hercules was able to do it! Hercules diverted two rivers that were nearby. They flooded the stables, washing the muck away.

Fun Fact: Eurystheus told Hercules that this labor was not successfully completed because the rivers did the work.

The Stymphalian Birds

The next labor was to kill the *Stymphalian (stim-fay-lee-an) Birds* of *Lake Stymphalia.* They were huge man-eating monsters with metallic wings and bronze beaks. Their dung was poisonous, and they could throw their feathers at people like knives. Hercules used a rattle to scare the birds from their hiding places. When they flew above, he shot them down with poisonous arrows.

The Cretan Bull

The seventh labor was to capture the *Cretan Bull.* The massive bull had been terrorizing the island of Crete and destroying their crops. Hercules captured the bull with his bare hands.

A statue of Hercules and the Cretan Bull.
(https://pixabay.com/photos/heracles-hercules-sculpture-bull-1374830/)

The Mares of Diomedes

The *Mares of Diomedes (dye-oh-mee-deez)* were a group of female horses that had been trained to eat human flesh by their owner, Diomedes. He was the king of *Thrace*. Because of this, they were incredibly dangerous. It was also said they could breathe fire.

Hercules asked his friend to help him steal the horses. However, King Diomedes chased after them. Hercules was forced to leave his friend alone with the mares while he fought the king's army. When Hercules returned, he discovered that the horses had eaten his friend. He fed the king to his own horses as revenge. After the horses had been fed they became calmer. This gave Hercules the opportunity to seal their mouths shut so they couldn't do more harm.

A drawing of Hercules with the Mares of Diomedes.

(https://commons.wikimedia.org/wiki/File:Hercules_and_the_Mares_of_Diomedes_LACMA_65.37.14.jpg)

The Girdle of Hippolyta

For his ninth task, King Eurystheus told Hercules to steal a *girdle* (a type of underwear worn around the waist like a corset) from the queen of the Amazons, *Hippolyta (huh-po-luh-tuh)*. The king's daughter wanted the girdle for herself. So, Eurystheus decided to send Hercules to take it since the Amazons were a fearsome tribe of warrior women.

When Hercules arrived at the home of the Amazons, Hippolyta agreed to give him her girdle. She had heard of his impressive achievements and wanted to form an alliance with him. Hercules invited her to have lunch on his ship, and she happily agreed.

While they were having lunch, Hera snuck onto the island and spread rumors about Hercules. She made the Amazons believe he had kidnapped their queen. So, they rode their horses to Hercules's ship to confront him. When Hercules saw the army of Amazons approaching, he mistakenly believed that Hippolyta had set a trap for him. Without thinking, he killed the queen and took the belt before sailing away.

The Cattle of Geryon

Hercules then had to steal the cattle belonging to a three-headed giant named *Geryon (jeeuh-ree-uhn)*, who lived on the island of Erytheia. Geryon had a two-headed dog and a man to help him guard his cattle. Hercules easily killed the dog and the guard with his club. Hercules was able to defeat Geryon by using arrows that he had dipped in the poisonous blood of the Lernaean Hydra.

Herding the cattle back proved to be almost as difficult as taking them in the first place. On Hercules's return home, a giant stole some of the

A drawing of Hercules herding the Cattle of Geryon.

cattle, and others ran away. It took Hercules more than a year to get them all back. But before he reached the king, another obstacle was thrown at him by Hera. She flooded the rivers. To reach home, Hercules had to create a bridge from rocks.

The Hesperidean Apples

Hercules's eleventh task was to steal golden apples from the garden of the Hesperides. The Hesperides were sunset nymphs, and the exact location of their garden was unknown. To find it, Hercules had to capture the shapeshifting *Old Man of the Sea* and get him to reveal where it was.

There are two different versions of how Hercules stole the apples. In one, he killed a dragon that was guarding the apples. In another, he tricked the god *Atlas*, the father of the nymphs, into getting the apples for him. In return, Hercules said he would take over Atlas's job of holding the heavens on his shoulders while he retrieved them. When Atlas returned with the apples, Hercules asked him to hold the skies while he adjusted his cloak. As soon as the heavens were back on Atlas's shoulders, Hercules escaped with the apples.

Once he showed the apples to King Eurystheus, Hercules returned them to the garden.

Cerberus, Guardian of the Underworld

Hercules's final task was to capture the three-headed dog, Cerberus, who guarded the gates to the underworld. Before Hercules could capture Cerberus, he would first need to learn how to travel between the earth and the underworld without dying. To get there, he would have to travel on the river *Acheron* to where Cerberus was. When

Hercules reached the underworld, he asked Hades for his permission to take Cerberus to King Eurystheus.

Hades agreed to let Hercules try and capture the fierce dog on one condition. He could not use any weapons or hurt Cerberus. Hercules made Cerberus fall asleep, and he took him. Cerberus began to wake up just as they arrived at King Eurystheus's chambers. In his usual cowardly fashion, the king hid in fear from the dog. He begged Hercules to take it back to Hades. He also finally agreed that Hercules had completed all of his tasks and was free.

A drawing of Hercules capturing Cerberus.

(Antonio Tempesta, CC0, via Wikimedia Commons https://commons.wikimedia.org/wiki/File:Hercules_
and_Cerberus-_Hercules_grasps_the_collar_of_Cerberus,_two_demons_appear_at_
left,_from_the_series_%27The_Labors_of_Hercules%27_MET_DP832522.jpg)

Chapter 5 Activity

Can you match the creatures of Hercules's twelve labors with their location?

Lion, Hydra, Boar, Birds, Bull, Cattle, Cerberus

Lerna, Mount Erymanthos, Crete, Nemea, Erytheia, Lake Stymphalia, the underworld

The Nemean Lion was from Nemea.

The Lernaean Hydra was from Lerna.

The Erymanthian Boar was from Mount Erymanthos.

The Stymphalian Birds were from Lake Stymphalia.

The Cretan Bull was from Crete.

The Geryon Cattle were from Erytheia.

Cerberus was guarding the gates of the underworld.

Chapter 6: Theseus and the Minotaur

Hercules wasn't the only Greek hero to have undertaken great quests. Another famous hero was *Theseus (thee-see-uhs)*. His mother was Princess *Aethra (ee-thra)* of *Troezen (tree-zen)*, and his father was the king of Athens, *Aegeus (ay-gee-uhs)*. King Aegeus visited Troezen on his way back from visiting an oracle. He had gone to the oracle for answers on whether he would ever have a son.

After spending the night with Aethra, Aegeus hid his sword and a pair of sandals under a huge rock. He told Aethra that if she gave birth to a son in nine months' time, she must wait until he was an adult and find out if he could lift the rock. If he was able to lift the rock, he should go to Athens with the sword and sandals. Aegeus would then know he was his true heir and the next king. When the time came, Theseus was able to lift the rock. He was ready to journey to Athens to claim his throne.

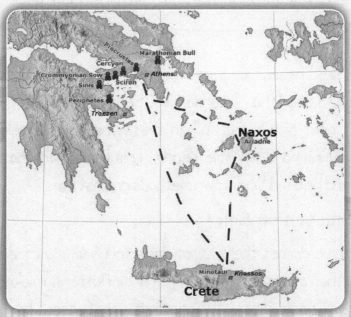

A map of Theseus's labors.
Credit: User:Future Perfect at Sunrise, CC0, via Wikimedia Commons;
(https://commons.wikimedia.org/wiki/File:Theseus_Map.jpg)

Fun Fact: Poseidon was also rumored to be Theseus's father, which would make Theseus a demigod.

Instead of heading straight to Athens, Theseus wanted to earn his father's respect by undertaking many heroic acts, just like his idol Hercules had.

Periphetes

The first challenge Theseus ran into was when he came across *Periphetes (puh-ree-fet-teez)*. He was a *brigand*, a bandit who would rob travelers. Periphetes carried a huge club made of bronze that he would beat travelers with. Periphetes was no match for Theseus, though. Theseus surprised Periphetes and took the club from him. Theseus then gave Periphetes a taste of his own medicine by using his weapon against him.

Fun Fact: Theseus kept the club and often used it.

Sinis

Not long after, Theseus encountered another bandit, *Sinis (see-neez)*. Sinis was nicknamed the "Pine Bender" because he would tie travelers up against bent pine trees. When these trees were released, the travelers suffered a horrible death. This bandit was no match for Theseus, and he used Sinis's own methods against him.

The Crommyonian Sow

Theseus came across the *Crommyonian (cruh-my-own-ee-an) Sow*. This was either a very large wild pig or an unflattering nickname for an unattractive female robber. Whichever it was, Theseus had no problem defeating them.

Sciron

The next brigand Theseus met was called *Sciron (sky-ron)*. Sciron would force people to wash his feet. When they were bent over, Sciron would kick them off the cliff edge into the sea, where they would be eaten by a giant turtle. Theseus didn't fall for this trick, though. He grabbed Sciron's foot and threw him off the cliff. He suffered the same fate as the poor travelers he had tricked.

Drawing of Theseus and Sciron.
(https://commons.wikimedia.org/wiki/File:Theseus_und_Stiron.jpg#file)

Cercyon

Next, Theseus was challenged to a wrestling match to the death by *Cercyon (ser-see-on)*. Of course, Cercyon was no match for Theseus.

Procrustes

Procrustes (pro-cruhsts) had an especially cruel and unusual way of tricking people to their deaths. He would kindly invite weary travelers to spend the night in his home. Then, he gave them the choice of two beds: one short and one long. Whichever the traveler chose, Procrustes would force their body to fit by hammering or stretching their limbs. Thankfully, Theseus was able to use Procrustes's own torture against him.

After defeating Procrustes, Theseus finally reached Athens. However, his challenges were not over. When he arrived, he was not recognized by Aegeus. The king's wife, the sorceress *Medea (muh-dee-uh)*, did recognize him. Medea did not want Theseus to become king instead of her son. She decided to send him on a deadly quest to kill the *Marathonian (mah-rah-thoh-nee-an) Bull*.

The Marathonian Bull

Fun Fact: The Marathonian Bull was the same bull that Hercules had captured in his seventh labor.

A painting of Theseus capturing the Marathonian Bull.
(https://commons.wikimedia.org/wiki/File:Theseus_Taming_the_Bull_of_Marathon_LACMA_M.2000.179.15.jpg)

The Cretan Bull became known as the Marathonian Bull since it now terrorized the people of Marathon. Theseus captured it and presented it to Medea and Aegeus. Then, he sacrificed it to Apollo so it couldn't escape and cause more damage.

Medea was furious to find that Theseus had survived. So, she decided she would poison his wine at the celebratory feast. Luckily, just as Theseus was about to drink the wine, Aegeus recognized his sword and sandals. He realized Theseus was his son and true heir. More importantly, he also discovered that his wife was trying to poison Theseus. He stopped his son from drinking the poison just in time. Aegeus then banished Medea forever and proclaimed Theseus as his rightful heir.

Even though Medea had been banished, this did not mean that Theseus's trials were over. Not long after, Aegeus had to go to Crete to pay tribute to the king there. To repay the king for his son being killed by the Athenians, Aegeus sent fourteen noble men and women every year

A postcard of Theseus and the Minotaur.

to Crete to meet the same fate. They would be thrown into a *labyrinth*, a type of maze that was made by a man named *Daedalus (dee-duh-luhs)*. Within the labyrinth was the *Minotaur*, a creature that was half-man and half-bull. It would eat anyone it encountered in the labyrinth.

Theseus decided he wanted to do something to put an end to the sacrifices. He volunteered to be one of the tributes. When they arrived in Crete, Princess *Ariadne (a-ree-ad-nee)* immediately fell in love with Theseus. She vowed to help him. In return, he promised he would marry her if he survived.

Ariadne convinced Daedalus to give her an enchanted ball of thread that would show Theseus the correct way out of the labyrinth. Theseus headed deep into the middle of the maze and found the Minotaur. He bravely fought the creature and defeated it before following the thread out of the labyrinth to safety.

A sculpture of Theseus killing the Minotaur.
(https://commons.wikimedia.org/wiki/File:Theseus_Slaying_Minotaur_by_Barye.jpg)

When Theseus emerged from the labyrinth unharmed, he took Ariadne with him. However, Theseus abandoned her on the way back to Athens. It is not clear why he did this.

Before Theseus left for Crete, he had promised his father that if he survived, he would change his ship's sails from black to white. However, he forgot to do this. When King Aegeus saw the ship approaching with black sails, he was heartbroken. He believed his son had died fighting the Minotaur. The forlorn king couldn't stand the grief and threw himself from the cliffs.

With his father gone, Theseus was crowned the new king of Athens. Theseus went on to be a very impressive ruler.

Chapter 6 Activity

1. Who was Theseus's father? How did he recognize Theseus as his legitimate heir?

2. Name two of the six villains Theseus killed on his way to Athens.

3. Who decided that Theseus should go and capture the Marathonian Bull?

4. Where was the Minotaur?

5. How did Theseus get out of the Minotaur's lair?

6. Why did Aegeus kill himself?

Chapter 6 Answer

1. **Who was Theseus's father? How did he recognize Theseus as his legitimate heir?**
   King Aegeus of Athens. Theseus was carrying the sword and sandals that the king had hidden under a rock.

2. **Name two of the six villains Theseus killed on his way to Athens.** Periphetes, Sinis, the Crommyonian Sow, Sciron, Cercyon, Procrustes.

3. **Who decided that Theseus should go and capture the Marathonian Bull?** Aegeus's wife, Medea.

4. **Where was the Minotaur? In a labyrinth in Crete.**

5. **How did Theseus get out of the Minotaur's lair? With a magical ball of thread.**

6. **Why did Aegeus kill himself? Because he thought Theseus was dead since his ship had black sails, not white.**

Chapter 7: Perseus and Medusa

We have already briefly mentioned Medusa. Now we are going to find out how and why she was killed by *Perseus*. Perseus was one of Zeus's many children. His mother was *Danae (duh-nay)*, the princess of *Argos*. Danae was imprisoned by her father because of a prophecy. It was said that one of her sons would kill the king. The king believed that if she was in prison, there was no possible way she could marry or fall pregnant.

However, the gods could still see her through a small crack in the roof. Zeus noticed Danae and was overcome by her beauty. One day, he transformed himself into golden rain so he could slip through the crack and meet her.

Just over nine months later, the king of Argos was shocked to discover that Danae was no longer alone in her cell. She had a brand-new baby in her arms! The king feared that the prophecy would come true, so he decided to get rid of Danae and Perseus. The king ordered his daughter and grandson to be locked inside a chest and thrown into the sea.

Luckily, the chest drifted to safety onto the island of *Seriphos*. Danae and Perseus lived there happily. Perseus grew up to be big and strong. Eventually, the king of Seriphos, *Polydectes (pol-ee-deck-teez)*, noticed Danae and fell madly in love. He asked her to marry him. Danae turned the king down, which he did not take well. He decided that her refusal was because of her son, so he decided to get rid of Perseus.

Polydectes pretended he was going to marry a different woman. Every citizen in Seriphos would have to give a horse as a gift for the wedding. Perseus could not afford a horse. He told the king he would bring him any other gift he wanted.

Polydectes couldn't believe his luck! He told Perseus to bring him the head of the Gorgon Medusa. The king did not expect Perseus to return. After all, Medusa was a fearsome monster with snakes for hair. She would turn people to stone if they looked in her eyes.

A sculpture of Medusa.
Credit: Metropolitan Museum of Art, CC0, via Wikimedia Commons;
(https://commons.wikimedia.org/wiki/File:Antefix,_head_of_Medusa_MET_DP-12520-001.jpg)

Perseus immediately encountered a problem. He could not find the Gorgon's lair! He searched for days. Finally, the gods decided they should help. Athena and Hermes advised Perseus to find the *Graeae (gra-ee)*, the sisters of the Gorgons. They also lent him Hermes's sickle and Athena's bronze shield.

The Graeae were three old women. They only had one eye and one tooth that they shared with each other. As one of the women passed the eye and tooth to another, Perseus grabbed them. He demanded that the women help him. The Graeae told him he must visit some nymphs who knew where the Gorgon's lair was.

The nymphs happily helped him, and they even gave him some useful items for his quest, such as winged sandals, a *kibisis* (an impenetrable bag), and Hades's helmet of invisibility.

Perseus used his new sandals to fly to the Gorgon's lair. Medusa was sleeping. Thanks to the invisibility helmet, Perseus was able to sneak up on her. Then, he used Athena's shield to look at the Gorgon's reflection. This way, he did not have to look directly at her. Before Medusa could realize what was happening, Perseus chopped off her head with Hermes's sickle. Even with her head cut off, Medusa's gaze could still turn him to stone. So, he quickly put the head in his kibisis, where it could do him no harm.

A sculpture of Perseus with Medusa's head.
(https://pixabay.com/photos/medusa-perseus-head-vatican-statue-1366362/)

When Perseus chopped off Medusa's head, a winged horse, *Pegasus*, and a soldier with a golden sword called *Chrysaor (kree-sour)* were born from her neck.

Fun Fact: Chrysaor is sometimes depicted as a flying boar.

With the head safely tucked away, Perseus was able to fly away on Pegasus's back.

A painting of Perseus and Pegasus.
(https://commons.wikimedia.org/wiki/File:Perseus_med_Medusahuvudet.jpg)

On the way back home, Perseus met the Titan Atlas, who held the heavens on his shoulders. Perseus took pity on him and decided to free Atlas of his pain by turning him to stone using Medusa's head.

Fun Fact: The Titan became the Atlas Mountains, which are in Africa.

As Perseus continued his travels, he met Princess *Andromeda*. The princess had been chained to a rock in the middle of the ocean to be eaten by a sea monster. Perseus fell in love with Andromeda. He asked her father if he could marry her in exchange for killing the monster. The king happily agreed, and Perseus rescued the princess and then married her.

When Perseus finally returned to Seriphos, he discovered the true reason Polydectes had sent him to kill Medusa. Enraged, Perseus turned the king and his men to stone with the Gorgon's head. Then, he gave the head to Athena as a thank you.

Fun Fact: Athena put Medusa's head on her shield.

Perseus planned to return home and make peace with his father. However, the prophecy still came true. Both men happened to be in the same place at the same time without either knowing. Perseus competed in an athletic contest, and he threw a discus that accidentally hit his father and killed him.

Chapter 7 Activity

Perseus's mother was _____ (Danae/Lydia/Demeter), and _____ (Hermes/Zeus/Poseidon) was his father. He was born in Argos, where his mother was imprisoned. They managed to escape to the island of _____ (Sifnos/Seriphos/Crete), where he was raised. King Polydectes gave him the quest of killing _____ (Minotaur/Hydra/Medusa) and bringing him her _____ (shield/head/hair). She was a monster whose hair was made of _____ (tentacles/snakes/stone). Whoever looked her in the eyes instantly turned to _____ (stone/snakes/crystals).

Before Perseus could kill the monster, he had to find the Gorgon's lair. He first asked the _____ (Graeae/Gorgons/King) and then the nymphs. The nymphs gave him some winged sandals, a kibisis, and _____ (Zeus's thunderbolts /Hades's helmet of invisibility/Poseidon's trident).

Perseus also received help from the gods Athena and _____ (Apollo/Hermes/Zeus). Hermes gave him his _____ (sword/knife/sickle) to chop off the Gorgon's head. Athena gave him her _____ (shield/helmet/bag), which he used to look at the Gorgon's reflection. When he cut off the monster's head, Chrysaor, a flying boar or soldier, and Pegasus, a flying (dog/bear/horse), were born. Perseus flew away to safety on Pegasus.

Perseus's mother was <u>Danae</u>, and <u>Zeus</u> was his father. He was born in Argos, where his mother was imprisoned. They managed to escape to the island of <u>Seriphos</u>, where he was raised. King Polydectes gave him the quest of killing Medusa and bringing him her head. She was a monster whose hair was made of <u>snakes</u>. Whoever looked her in the eyes instantly turned to <u>stone</u>.

Before Perseus could kill the monster, he had to find the Gorgon's lair. He first asked the <u>Graeae</u> and then the nymphs. The nymphs gave him some winged sandals, a kibisis, and <u>Hades's helmet of invisibility</u>.

Perseus also received help from the gods Athena and <u>Hermes</u>. Hermes gave him his <u>sickle</u> to chop off the Gorgon's head. Athena gave him her <u>shield</u>, which he used to look at the Gorgon's reflection. When he cut off the monster's head, Chrysaor, a flying boar or soldier, and Pegasus, a flying <u>horse</u>, were born. He flew away to safety on Pegasus.

Chapter 8: Jason and the Argonauts

The next Greek hero we are going to learn about is Jason. He was a mortal prince and the son of King *Aeson (ay-son)* of *Iolcus*. The king's brother, *Pelias (pel-ee-uhs)*, *usurped* him, which means he took over the throne. He also killed all of Aeson's children so he would have no heirs. However, Pelias incorrectly believed that Jason had been stillborn. Aeson knew that Pelias would kill Jason if he discovered the truth. Aeson sent his son to live with the centaur *Chiron (kai-ruhn)*. Chiron raised Jason and taught him how to be a strong and brave man. During this time, Pelias visited an oracle, who told him that he should be careful of a man wearing one sandal.

When Jason was an adult, he decided to return to Iolcus to take part in some games that were being held. On his way, Jason met the goddess Hera and helped her to cross a river. While he was helping her, his sandal slipped off and was carried away down the river. Hera secretly blessed Jason since she was angry with Pelias for not honoring her. She planned to help Jason become king and overthrow Pelias.

When Jason arrived in Iolcus, he introduced himself to Pelias as the rightful heir to the throne. Pelias was horrified, especially because of the oracle's prediction. He decided he would get rid of Jason by sending him on an impossible quest. Pelias told Jason that if he was able to bring him the *Golden Fleece*, which was the skin of a special ram in *Colchis*, he would step down from the throne. Jason agreed and set out on his mission.

A drawing of Jason meeting King Pelias.
Internet Archive Book Images, No restrictions, via Wikimedia Commons
(https://commons.wikimedia.org/wiki/File:The_golden_fleece_and_
the_heroes_who_lived_before_Achilles_(1921)_(14580243159).jpg)

Unlike many other Greek heroes, Jason decided to assemble a group of brave heroes to help him. Together, these heroes were known as the Argonauts.

Fun Fact: In some versions of this myth, there are as many as fifty Argonauts! The most famous one was Hercules.

The Argonauts were named after their ship, the *Argo*. The ship was given its name for two reasons. First, Argos built it. Second, the Greek word *argos* means "swift" or "fast."

The Argo had a whopping fifty oars to propel it!

The *Argo* was no ordinary ship. It was built with the help of the goddesses Hera and Athena. It had special powers thanks to its wood, which was taken from the oak trees in the sacred forest of *Dodona (duh-doh-nuh).*

The ship's powers were said to include the ability to talk and even make prophecies!

The first place the Argonauts visited was the island of *Lemnos*, which was inhabited only by women. The women had killed all of the men because of a curse that made the women smell bad. These men left their wives for other women, which drove the women insane. While on the island, the Argonauts had many children with the women, creating a new race called *Minyans.*

Next, they went to the *Doliones (dol-yoh-nez).* While many of the group were away hunting for supplies, their ship was attacked by a

A map of the Argo's route.
(https://commons.wikimedia.org/wiki/File:Argonauts_Georgia_1988.jpg)

group of giants with six arms called the *Gegeines (gey-gaynes)*. Luckily, Hercules was still on board. He was able to kill many of the Gegeines before the Argonauts returned.

Sadly, as they were leaving that night, their boat was blown back to shore. The Doliones mistakenly attacked, thinking they were pirates. The fight ended with the death of the Doliones king. When the Argonauts realized their mistake, they held a funeral for the king.

The Argonauts then traveled to *Salmydessus (sal-mee-dee-sos)* in Thrace. Here, they met King *Phineus (fin-ee-uhs)*. Phineus had been blinded by Zeus for using his gift of prophecy to reveal a secret plan. As further punishment, Zeus sent the *Harpies*, who were birds with human faces. They tormented Phineus by stealing his food before he could eat it. Jason and the Argonauts took pity on the king and decided to help. They lured the Harpies to fly down with a huge feast. Then, the *Boreads (bor-ee-adz)*, the wind gods, blew them away for good.

Phineus was so grateful for their help that he told the Argonauts how they could get to Colchis and how they would be able to pass the *Symplegades (simp-lah-ge-deez)*. The Symplegades were cliffs that moved and crushed sailors as they tried to pass between them. Phineas told Jason to release a dove. If it got through, the boat would be able to pass. The dove survived with only minor injuries, and so did the *Argo*.

Finally, they arrived in Colchis and were greeted by King *Aeetes (ay-ee-tee)*. The golden ram belonged to the king. He told Jason he would give the ram to him if he could complete some impossible tasks in just one day. Jason was disheartened. He feared he would leave empty-handed. Luckily, Hera stepped in to help. She managed to get Eros to shoot the king's daughter, Medea, with his arrow so she would fall in love with

Jason. As you may remember, Medea was a powerful sorceress. With her help, Jason could face the challenges.

His first task was to plow a field using two fire-breathing bulls called the *Khalkotauroi (cal-co-tauh-roy)*. Medea gave Jason a magical cream that made him invulnerable to fire. He was able to complete the task without a problem.

Next, Jason had to plant some dragon's teeth into the newly plowed field. Although he managed this easily, an army of stone soldiers appeared from the ground when the last tooth was planted. Medea told Jason to throw a rock into the middle of the warriors. This confused them. They did not know who had thrown it, and they began to fight among themselves. By sunset, Jason was the only one left alive.

A drawing of Jason, Medea, and the Golden Fleece.
(https://commons.wikimedia.org/wiki/File:The_golden_fleece_and_the
_heroes_who_lived_before_Achilles_(1921)_(14766908825).jpg)

Even though Jason had completed his tasks before the end of the day, Aeetes did not want to give up the Golden Fleece. So, he planned to kill Jason while he slept that night. Fearing this, Medea led Jason to the tree where the Golden Fleece was being guarded by a dragon. Medea cast a spell on the dragon to make it fall asleep so Jason could grab the Golden Fleece.

As they were escaping Colchis, Medea showed her devotion to Jason. She killed her own brother to stop her father from following them. On their journey home, the Argonauts encountered many dangers, one of which Medea was responsible for stopping. She killed the giant bronze man, *Talos (tah-loss)*, who threw stones at people approaching Crete.

Fun Fact: The Argonauts also passed by the Sirens, who lured sailors to their deaths with their beautiful voices. Luckily, the poet Orpheus was on the boat. He played his lyre so loudly that the men could not hear the Sirens' deadly song.

By the time Jason made it home, he was horrified to see how much his father had aged. He begged Medea to help him give some of his own life to his father. Medea would not do this. Instead, she cut the old man and removed all his old blood. She replaced it with an *elixir* of youth. When Aeson woke up, he was forty years younger.

When Pelias's daughters heard of this, they asked Medea to do the same for their father. Encouraged by Hera, Medea told the daughters she would do the same ritual. However, she did not resurrect the king. With Pelias now dead, his son became king. He banished Jason and Medea.

Although Medea had been faithful to Jason, he did not return her love.

He later fell in love with another woman. The heartbroken Medea got her revenge. She killed Jason's new love. She also killed her own sons that she had with Jason. Medea knew this would cause him unbearable pain.

Fun Fact: Hera no longer supported Jason after his betrayal of Medea.

In some stories, it is said that Jason killed himself since he could not bear the loss. In others, he lived longer and finally claimed his throne. Sadly, in the stories where he had a long life, it was an unhappy one. He also did not have a hero's death. He was sleeping on the rotting *Argo* when a beam broke off and crushed him.

Chapter 8 Activity

Can you tell which statements are true or false?

1. Jason was educated by Pelias.

2. Pelias was Jason's father.

3. The *Argo* was the name of Jason's ship.

4. The Golden Fleece was a ram's skin.

5. Hera helped Jason because she was in love with him.

6. Jason's ship had special powers because it was built with sacred oak.

7. Medea helped Jason get the Golden Fleece.

8. The Golden Fleece was guarded by a three-headed dog.

Chapter 8 Answer

1. Jason was educated by Pelias. False.
   He was educated by the centaur Chiron.

2. Pelias was Jason's father. False.
   His father was Aeson.

3. The Argo was the name of Jason's ship. True.

4. The Golden Fleece was a ram's skin. True.

5. Hera helped Jason because she was in love with him. False.
   Hera helped Jason out of revenge against Pelias. Medea was the one who helped him out of love.

6. Jason's ship had special powers because it was built with sacred oak. True.

7. Medea helped Jason get the Golden Fleece. True.

8. The Golden Fleece was guarded by a three-headed dog. False.
   The Golden Fleece was guarded by a dragon.

Chapter 9: The Trojan War

Although there are many battles and wars in Greek mythology, the most famous by far must be the *Trojan War*. The war took place between the *Achaeans (a-kee-ans)* of *Achaea (a-kee-ah)* and the *Trojans* from the city of *Troy*.

Fun Fact: The Greek soldiers lay siege on the city of Troy for over ten years!

The fighting between the Achaeans began during a wedding feast. The goddess of *strife* (conflict and disagreements) was upset that she was not invited. She threw her gift into the crowd of guests. The gift was a golden apple with the words "For the fairest of all" carved into it.

Three goddesses, Hera, Aphrodite, and Athena, began to argue. Each of them believed they were the most beautiful. When they were unable to reach an agreement, they asked Zeus to decide. Zeus wisely realized that he would upset the goddesses he didn't pick. So, he asked the young prince of Troy, *Paris*, to decide instead.

Paris was struck by their beauty, and he could not decide. So, the goddesses began to make him promises if he chose them. Athena offered to make him a skilled and wise warrior. Hera promised him power and land. Aphrodite said she would give him the most beautiful woman in the world, *Helen of Sparta*. Paris chose Aphrodite.

Word of Helen's beauty had spread, and she had many noblemen lining up to ask for her hand in marriage. Her father, the king of Sparta, was struggling to decide who he should choose to marry his daughter. He did not want to create enemies by picking the wrong husband. The wisest of the suitors, *Odysseus*, told the king he would help him in return for c marriage to his niece. The king agreed. Odysseus told him the men must swear an oath to protect Helen and her husband no matter what the final decision was. Once this had been done, the king chose a man called Menelaus (meh-nuh-lay-uhs) to marry Helen.

Not long after the wedding, Menelaus had to go to a funeral in Crete. While he was away, Aphrodite decided to sneak Paris into Sparta to meet Helen. Once inside the palace, Aphrodite used her influence and Eros's arrows to make Helen fall in love with Paris. Helen spent the night with Paris. In the morning, they eloped for Troy.

A carving of Helen of Sparta.
(https://commons.wikimedia.org/wiki/File:Helene_Paris_Louvre_K6.jpg)

When Menelaus returned home to discover his new bride gone, he decided to call upon the other suitors to keep their promise. Menelaus and his powerful brother, King *Agamemnon (a-guh-mem-non)* of

Mycenae, immediately set off to recruit more men. They headed to Troy to rescue Helen.

When the Greek men arrived at Odysseus's home, he did not want to leave. His son was only one year old, and he knew from an oracle that if he left, he would not return for many years. So, he pretended to be insane. He plowed his field with salt using a donkey and an ox. One of the men saw through this trick and placed Odysseus's son in front of the plow. Odysseus had no choice but to leave. He also knew from the oracle that the Greeks could not win without one man, *Achilles (uh-ki-leez)*.

When Achilles was a baby, his mother believed he would either live a long and boring life or die young and heroically in battle. To prevent this, she took him to the *River Styx* that ran through the underworld. She held him by the ankle and dipped him in the water to make him invulnerable.

Fun Fact: Achilles' heel was the only part that was not protected. This led to his eventual downfall. That is why the phrase "Achilles' heel" is still used today to describe someone's one weakness.

With Achilles on board, the Achaeans set sail for Troy. However, they did not know the way. They ended up going too far and landed in a place called *Mysia (mi-see-uh)*. This land was ruled by King *Telephus (tell-uh-fuhs)*, who was one of Hercules's sons. During a battle there, Achilles proved his impressive strength by killing many men. He even managed to hurt Telephus.

Fun Fact: Achilles was only fifteen years old when he bested Telephus!

Even though they knew how to find Troy now, the Achaeans still couldn't get there. Artemis was stopping the wind. She was punishing Agamemnon for killing a sacred deer. She demanded that he sacrifice his own daughter for them to continue their journey.

Achilles and Agamemnon.
(https://commons.wikimedia.org/wiki/File:Achilles_Agamemnon_
Pompei_mosaic_NAMNaples_10006.jpg)

When they finally reached Troy, none of the men wanted to be the first to leave the boat. This was because an oracle had predicted that the first Greek to step foot on Trojan soil would be the first to die. *Protesilaus (pro-ti-suh-lay-uhs)* bravely volunteered. He was killed in a one-on-one fight with Troy's beloved prince and favorite fighter, Hector.

After almost ten years of war, the tensions in the Greek camp were running high. After a falling out with Agamemnon, Achilles refused to fight. Without their strongest warrior, the Greeks began to lose. *Patroclus*, who was a good friend of Achilles, decided he would lead the army disguised as Achilles. Believing their fearless leader had returned, the Achaeans managed to push the Trojans back.

Hector saw his opportunity to kill Achilles and challenged him to a fight. Hector did indeed win. When he removed his opponent's helmet, he was shocked to find he had killed Patroclus.

A statue of Menelaus carrying the dead Patroclus.

When Achilles heard of Patroclus's death, he immediately rejoined the fight. Hector knew that the wrath of Achilles would be great. He also knew he was unlikely to win in a fight against him. Therefore, Hector went to the palace to say goodbye to his wife and young son, fearing that he would not see them again.

Hector says goodbye to his family.

Credit: Benjamin West, CC0, via Wikimedia Commons; https://commons.wikimedia.org/wiki/File: Hector_taking_leave_of_Andromache-_the_Fright_of_Astyanax_MET_DP821060.jpg

Eventually, Achilles found Hector. They fought, and, as expected, Achilles won. Achilles gloated over his victory. He dragged the beloved prince's body behind his chariot outside of the city's walls. The king of

Achilles dragging Hector's body

Credit: Chcncc67789, CC BY-SA 4.0 https://creativecommons.org/licenses/by-sa/4.0 via Wikimedia Commons; https://commons.wikimedia.org/wiki/File:Triumph_of_Achilles_by_Franz_von_Matsch.jpg

Troy visited Achilles in secret to make a heartfelt plea for his son to be buried properly. Achilles then gave the body to the Trojans.

Fun Fact: The Trojans would get their revenge for Achilles's act. Hector's own brother, Paris, would kill the mighty Achilles with a single arrow. The arrow hit Achilles in the heel—his one weak spot.

Odysseus finally came up with a plan that would win the battle for the Greeks. He said they needed to build a giant, hollow wooden horse. A group of Achaean soldiers hid inside it while the rest of the Greek army retreated. A man named *Sinon (sigh-non)* stayed behind to present the *Trojan Horse* to the king of Troy. He said it was an offering for Athena and a token of their surrender.

The people of Troy gladly accepted the gift, even though they were warned by the priests and priestesses not to bring the Trojan Horse inside. Later that night, while the people of Troy slept, the soldiers inside the horse snuck out and opened the gates. The rest of the Greek army came inside the city's walls and made quick work of the unsuspecting Trojans. This ended the war for good.

A replica of the Trojan Horse.

Can you circle the correct word?

1. Agamemnon was the king of Troy/**Mycenae**.

2. Helen was married to **Menelaus**/Achilles.

3. Patroclus was Achilles's cousin/**best friend**.

4. Menelaus was **Agamemnon's**/Hector's brother.

5. Achilles killed **Hector**/Paris.

Chapter 9 Answer

1. Agamemnon was the king of Mycenae.

2. Helen was married to Menelaus.

3. Patroclus was Achilles's best friend.

4. Menelaus was Agamemnon's brother.

5. Achilles killed Hector.

Chapter 10: The Odyssey

This next story follows Odysseus on his journey home after the Trojan War. Although he had already been away from home for a long time, it would take him ten more years to finally reach *Ithaca*.

Fun Fact: Odysseus's journey is famously known because of an epic poem called the Odyssey by the ancient Greek poet Homer.

After winning the Trojan War, Odysseus and his twelve ships left Troy and headed for home. A strong wind blew the ships off course, and they landed among the *Cicones (si-koh-nee)*, who were allies of Troy. After winning a battle against the Cicones, Odysseus and his men got drunk on wine and stayed too long. This gave the Cicones time to gather more men and drive them away.

Odysseus lost three more men in the "land of the Lotus-Eaters." Here, some scouts were sent to check the area. They never returned because they ate the lotus. Anyone who ate the lotus would no longer care about returning home and wanted to stay to eat more.

Next, the ships arrived on the island of the Cyclopes. They ended up in the cave of the Cyclops *Polyphemus (po-luh-fee-muhs)*. The Cyclops was able to eat six men before Odysseus stepped in. He told Polyphemus that his name was "Nobody" and gave the Cyclops lots of wine. Once Polyphemus was drunk, Odysseus attacked and stabbed him in the eye. However, when the Cyclops cried out for help, he shouted that "Nobody" was attacking him. Of course, the other Cyclopes did not come to help. Odysseus and his remaining men were able to escape by hiding under Polyphemus's sheep.

When Polyphemus discovered Odysseus's real name, he asked his father, Poseidon, to punish Odysseus. Poseidon's wrath was the main reason it took Odysseus so long to get home.

Odysseus and Polyphemus.
(https://commons.wikimedia.org/wiki/File:Cyclops_and_Odysseus_vase_painting.svg)

After narrowly escaping the Cyclopes, Odysseus's ships arrived on an island belonging to *Aeolus (ay-oh-los)*, the god of wind. The men lived on the island for a month. Aeolus happily sent them on their way with a parting gift, a bag containing every wind except for the west wind.

For nine days, the ships safely floated toward Ithaca. But on the tenth day, Odysseus fell asleep, leaving the bag unattended. One of his men decided to peek inside the bag. As soon as the bag was opened, the winds were all released. The boat was violently thrown back to Aeolus. Aeolus realized Odysseus must be cursed and refused to help again.

Fun Fact: Odysseus then lost all of his ships but his own to man—eating giants!

After this, Odysseus's lone ship reached the island of *Aeaea (ay-ee-ah)*. It was ruled by a powerful witch named *Circe (ser-see)*. Circe turned the men into pigs. Odysseus was not changed, though. He had eaten a magical herb to protect him from magic. Odysseus defended his men, and she fell in love with him. She changed the pigs back into men. Odysseus decided to stay on the island as Circe's lover for one year.

A painting of Circe.
(https://commons.wikimedia.org/wiki/File:Circe_Offering_the_Cup_to_Odysseus.jpg)

Before leaving, Circe told Odysseus to visit an oracle of Hades. While in the underworld, Odysseus saw many of his old friends who had died in battle. He also saw his mother. She warned him that he must return home as quickly as he could because his wife was being courted by many suitors who believed Odysseus was dead.

Not long after leaving Aeaea, Odysseus's ship passed the Sirens. Luckily, Circe had warned him of how to evade the lure of the Sirens' song. The men stuffed their ears with beeswax. The beeswax was not enough to protect the men from hearing their songs, so the men also tied themselves down. This meant they couldn't escape when they were entranced by the song.

A painting of Odysseus and the Sirens.
(https://commons.wikimedia.org/wiki/File:WATERHOUSE_-_Ulises_y_las_Sirenas_(National_Gallery_of_Victoria,_Melbourne,_1891._%C3%93leo_sobre_lienzo,_100.6_x_202_cm).jpg)

Next, the ship had to sail through a narrow passage with two monsters on either side. On one side was *Charybdis (kuh-rib-duhs)*, a monster that created a whirlpool. On the other was *Scylla (si-luh)*, a female monster with twelve feet and six heads on snake-like necks. By trying to avoid one monster, a ship would have no choice but to face the other. The ship managed to pass, but they lost six men to Scylla.

The men's next stop was the island of *Thrinacia (thruh-nee-shuh)*, where the sun god, *Helios (hee-lee-os)*, kept his cattle. Although Odysseus warned his men not to eat the cattle, they did so anyway. Helios was angry, and he asked Zeus to punish the men. If Zeus did not, Helios said he would take the sun with him to the underworld. Zeus sent a massive storm that destroyed the ship and killed everyone apart from Odysseus.

The shipwrecked Odysseus washed up on the shores of *Ogygia (oh-ji-gee-uh)*, where he was found by a sorceress named *Calypso*. Calypso fell in love with Odysseus and decided to keep him as her prisoner. To try and make him stay, she offered him immortality. The homesick Odysseus refused. After seven long years, the gods took pity on him. Zeus and Hermes helped to free him.

After escaping Calypso, Odysseus reached the island of the *Phaeacians (fhay-ay-shuns)*. The Phaeacians were happy to help him get home and gave him a boat.

Fun Fact: The Phaeacians lived on the modern-day island of Corfu.

Finally, after many years of traveling, Odysseus reached Ithaca. With the help of Athena, he disguised himself as a beggar so he could sneak around without being discovered. Odysseus went straight to his faithful servant's house. While there, he bumped into his son, *Telemachus (tuh-leh-muh-kuhs)*, who was now a grown man.

The men headed to court, where the suitors were trying to marry *Penelope*, Odysseus's wife. The other suitors jeered and threw things at the disguised Odysseus. When Penelope entered, she announced that she was finally ready to marry one of the men. She said she would marry whoever could string Odysseus's bow and fire twelve arrows with it. As you might expect, no one could do that apart from the beggar. Odysseus then triumphantly removed his disguise and killed the suitors.

A drawing of Odysseus and Penelope meeting again
(https://commons.wikimedia.org/wiki/File:Schmied_illustration_Odyss%
C3%A9e-CompBibliophilesAutoClubFrance-1932vol3p173.png)

When Penelope first heard the news, she could not believe it. She was still in disbelief even after seeing him for herself. She shyly asked Odysseus if they could move their marriage bed into another room. Odysseus told her that he could not do this. One of the legs of the bed was an olive tree that was deeply rooted in the ground. He knew this because he had built it. The faithful Penelope realized that this must be her husband, for no other man had seen her bed. She was finally convinced this truly was her husband.

Chapter 10 Activity

Can you match the name with its corresponding phrase?

Penelope	helped Odysseus return home.
Calypso	was a Cyclops.
Polyphemus	turned Odysseus's men into pigs.
Circe	was Odysseus's wife.
The Phaeacians	gave Odysseus a bag of wind.
Aeolus	held Odysseus captive on her island for seven years.

Penelope	was Odysseus's wife.
Calypso	held Odysseus captive on her island for seven years.
Polyphemus	was a Cyclops.
Circe	turned Odysseus's men into pigs.
The Phaeacians	helped Odysseus return home.
Aeolus	gave Odysseus a bag of wind.

Bibliography

If you enjoyed this book, check out some of these other great resources for Greek mythology.

Websites:

"Greek Mythology."

https://www.ducksters.com/history/ancient_greek_mythology.php

"5 Terrifying Tales from Greek Mythology."

https://www.natgeokids.com/uk/discover/history/greece/greek-myths/

Videos:

"Top 19 Greek Gods and Goddesses Who Ruled Olympus."

https://www.youtube.com/watch?v=WM4KCHeEaoE. Created April 2018.

Books:

Ingri and Edgar Parin d'Aulaire. *D'Aulaires' Book of Greek Myths*. 1967.

Donna Jo Napoli. *Treasury of Greek Mythology: Classic Stories of Gods, Goddesses, Heroes & Monsters*. 2011.

Richard Marcus, Natalie Buczynsky & Jonathan Shelnutt. *Introduction to Greek Mythology for Kids*. 2021.

Jan Bajtlik. *Greek Myths and Mazes*. 2019.

DK and Jean Menzies. *Greek Myths: Meet the Heroes, Gods, and Monsters of Ancient Greece*. 2020.

Made in the USA
Las Vegas, NV
17 August 2022

53422457R00057